BRANCH LINES
TO MIDHURST

First published 1981
Reprinted 1982
Reprinted 1983

ISBN 0 906520 01 0

© *Middleton Press, 1981*

Published by Middleton Press
Easebourne Lane
Midhurst, West Sussex
GU29 9AZ

Printed & bound by Biddles Ltd,
Guildford and King's Lynn

INTRODUCTION

The railways to Midhurst had few individual characteristics of their own but were typical branch lines of the empires of the old companies. Scenically the east-west line had the advantage of running for its entire length along the Rother Valley, parallel to the South Downs whose silhouette could usually be enjoyed against the ever changing sky. The line from the south crossed the Downs by means of numerous cuttings and tunnels which often interrupted the view, but the vista from the occasional embankment more than compensated for this.

The authors have drawn upon the work of a large number of railway photographers, as the captions indicate, but despite having a combined collection of over 700 views, there are remarkably few of trains in the countryside. This may have been due to their infrequency. However there are numerous views of steam in action at the stations together with many details of architecture, operation and life on the railway.

Keith Smith, a dedicated model railway enthusiast, has lived in West Sussex all his life and on deciding to model some local stations found a severe deficiency in published material. Prolonged detective work revealed much useful information and led to an extensive collection of photographs of the lines.

In the early 1950's Vic Mitchell, was involved in the founding of the Festiniog Railway Society and also made many devious journeys by rail between London and the South Coast via Midhurst. Having now lived in that town for the past 20 years, he has also made a collection of local railway material.

This album results from combining these resources in an attempt to give pleasure to those who love our lost railways and those with an interest in the history of the locality. The stimulus to publish has been the centenary of the opening of the last railway to Midhurst, in 1881, and the book is, in part, a tribute to the engineers of that great Victorian expansionist age.

The album is divided into four sections — covering the lines from the east, west and south and finally Midhurst itself.

The authors would like to acknowledge the help and information received from:–

> J. Bragg, B.R. (Southern Region), H.C. Cooper, G. Evans, D. Fereday-Glenn, A. Flexman, Mrs M. Greenfield, E. Godfrey, A. Hill, H.R.H. Harmer (Chichester Library), L.C.G. Holden, L. Horwood, A.J. Hoskins, P. Hounsham, E. Liddle, D. Lannoway, Mrs S. Montgomery, I. Paget, Mrs G.J. Smith, J. Tullett, Mrs E. Wallis, West Sussex Record Office, Hugh Smith, Neil Stanyon, and particularly Paul Clark, Peter Jerrome and David Wallis.

The map and locomotive notes are reproduced by courtesy of the Railway Magazine and the drawings of Midhurst station and signalboxes were produced by Paul Newham. The "notice of opening" at the start of the Chichester section is from the library of J.T. Howard-Turner, the other section introductions being taken from a guide to Midhurst published in 1910. Copies of tickets have kindly been provided by N.C. Langridge and J. Hall.

To paint a picture of the development of Railways to Midhurst, it is first necessary to look at the mid-nineteenth century frame in which the scene is to be set.

The first line to enter the district was opened in stages by the London, Brighton and South Coast Railway Company from Brighton, westwards towards Portsmouth, reaching Chichester in 1847.

The rival company, the London and South Western Railway, completed its direct Portsmouth line by linking Godalming and Havant via Petersfield in 1859. This gave rise to the famous Battle of Havant, when the loyal workers (or 'navvies' as they were still called long after the canal building era) belonging to the rival companies set upon one another when the first direct train from Waterloo attempted, unsuccessfully, to reach Portsmouth.

Approach from the east

To the east, the L.B.S.C.R. began to open up virgin country by extending its branch from Three Bridges to Horsham and on towards Petworth by way of Pulborough. Although these were both small towns at the time the line opened on October 10th, 1859, the promoters sought wealth not from the limited number of passengers that might be forthcoming, but from freight carriage, both to and from the surrounding districts.

Although the inhabitants of Billingshurst were provided with a station from the outset, the residents of Fittleworth had to wait a further thirty years for trains to stop there. The present main line to the coast through Arundel was not opened until 1863.

"Petworth for Midhurst" was a truly rural terminal station situated almost two miles south of Petworth, but six miles east of Midhurst. The picturesqueness of this station obviously pleased the reporter from the 'West Sussex Gazette' who was present at the opening of the line. He later wrote, "The little station, which is built of polished deal, lies nestling under the hill in all the pride of perfect security. The railway buildings here are very numerous. There is

also a pretty little engine house for pumping up the water into a tank to supply the engines."

A fresh Act of Parliament was required to extend the line over the short distance to Midhurst. This was given the lengthy title of "Mid-Sussex and Midhurst Junction Railway." Its construction period was also lengthy – more than seven years – and when the line opened on October 15th, 1866, a local journalist headed a very brief article in the 'West Sussex Gazette,' "Wonders will never cease." At least one person was pleased with the opening, as, for many years, Thomas Maides, a newsagent in West Street, Midhurst, had made his newspaper boy walk in the early dawn along the unfinished railway to and from Petworth to fetch the daily news. The Act of Parliament had stipulated that an intermediate station should be constructed at Selham; however, it was almost six years later, in July, 1872, that this station opened.

Arrival from the west

Meanwhile, to the west of Midhurst, the battle for territory was successfully won by the L.S.W.R., whose line from Petersfield to Midhurst was opened on September 1st, 1864. In fact, a truce boundary had been agreed in 1860 by the two rival companies. This new branch had two intermediate stations, Elsted and Rogate & Harting, both of which were situated approximately a mile from the communities they served. The Midhurst terminus was described in the first South Western timetable as 'station for Petworth' despite the fact that the competitors' trains terminated several miles nearer to that town!

After the L.B.S.C.R. trains reached Midhurst, this small country town of some 1400 inhabitants could boast of having two railway termini situated a mere ½ mile to the south of the town. The two stations were sited a short distance apart on opposite sides of a minor country road leading to Bepton. A short connection constructed between the two stations was opened on December 17th, 1866, but, owing to the weakness of the bridge over

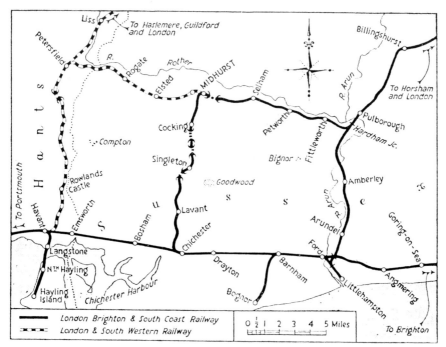

Map of the railways in the Midhurst area, showing pregrouping ownership

the Bepton Road, locomotives were prohibited from crossing it. This meant that it was used only for the transfer of freight. Wagons were either drawn across by horse or loose shunted by a locomotive (a practice known as 'fly-shunting'). A covered footway was provided on the north side of the bridge in an attempt to reduce the inconvenience to through passengers, who were forced to change trains at Midhurst.

Up from the south

Chichester's rail link with Midhurst was started in 1865 and the events leading up to the commencement of this work are well documented in Paul Clark's information book, "The Chichester and Midhurst Railway." Owing to financial problems, construction soon came to a halt and by 1868 work had stopped completely. The scheme was revived in 1876 when the L.B.S.C.R. decided to incorporate the Chichester to Midhurst line with their own Pulborough to Midhurst line. Contracts with the builder were exchanged in January, 1879. In view of the new plan, it was decided that the junction at Midhurst should now face towards Petworth. This

necessitated the building of a new station ½ mile to the east of the existing two termini. It also meant an even longer walk for passengers transferring between the two companies. In view of this a new road was built — New Road to this day.

The flamboyant architectural style employed on the new stations on this line was also used by the L.B.S.C.R. on its new lines in East Sussex, good examples remaining today on the Bluebell Railway. Generous station facilities were provided at Cocking, Singleton and Lavant but the all timber station buildings provided between Midhurst and Pulborough were of a style little used elsewhere in this County. Conversely the L.S.W.R. station buildings at Rogate, Elsted and Midhurst were almost identical, each having mainly round-headed windows, characteristic of many other stations on that company's system.

After the grouping of railway companies in 1923, the Southern Railway became responsible for all three lines to Midhurst and, after strengthening the Bepton Road bridge, it was able, from 12th July, 1925, to run trains from Petersfield into the former L.B.S.C.R. station, where a bay platform already existed to receive such trains. The L.S.W.R. station at Midhurst was closed to passenger traffic at the same time, but the goods sidings were retained. Other economy measures, such as the elimination of passing loops and staff reductions, were soon introduced at other stations.

Road transport competition in the early thirties meant yet further economies, the most notable of which was the withdrawal of regular passenger services between Chichester and Midhurst on 6th July, 1935. During World War II services were disrupted somewhat, since the tunnels on the line were used for the storage of ammunition trains on route to Portsmouth! After the War substantial freight traffic continued to be carried until through traffic was abruptly halted on 19th November, 1951, when the daily goods train from Chichester dropped into a stream just south of Midhurst after the culvert had been washed out in a storm. Freight services to Cocking and Singleton ceased after the complete closure of both stations on 28th August, 1953. Lavant Station, however, remained open and in 1954 the north end of the platform was surfaced in concrete to facilitate the loading of sugar beet and, between 1963 and 1970 when the station closed completely, Lavant was the central loading point for this traffic from about a ten mile radius.

Passenger services between Pulborough and Petersfield last ran on 5th February, 1955, and all traffic west of Midhurst also ceased after that day. An occasional special train appeared for the benefit of ramblers or railway enthusiasts, but otherwise goods trains only came to Midhurst until the final 'special' left on 18th October, 1964. Goods facilities had already been withdrawn from Fittleworth and Selham in May, 1963, but Petworth survived until 20th May, 1966.

In 1972 gravel extraction started to the south west of Lavant and a condition of the planning consent was that the material should be removed by rail. Special loading facilities were built south of Lavant and the unwashed gravel taken in a block train of bogie hopper wagons to the washing and screening plant about two miles east of Chichester. This short section of line is all that remains today of what must once have been a most picturesque railway route.

Strangely all the station buildings still survive to this day with the exception of the Midhurst L.B.S.C.R. station which was demolished to make way for housing development.

Locomotive variety

Motive power on the Midhurst branches has shown little variety. J. C. Craven, Locomotive Superintendent of the LBSCR from 1852 to 1869, had the odd practice of designing different locomotives for each individual branch line. Unfortunately, his first engine for the Midhurst branch, a double-framed 0-4-2 tank, No. 213, built in 1865, proved too heavy for the line and was transferred elsewhere. Older Craven engines had to work the line until October, 1866, when No. 230, a smaller 0-4-2 tank, was completed. This engine lasted until 1881, by which time Stroudley's famous Terrier 0-6-0 tanks had appeared; No. 42, *Tulsehill*, and No. 77, *Wonersh,* were familiar engines at Midhurst shed for many years. They were in turn replaced by Stroudley D1 class 0-4-2 tanks, of which the last survivor in passenger service, No. 2252, continued to appear on the branch until shortly before its withdrawal in 1950. The LBSCR shed at Midhurst was closed soon after grouping after which Horsham shed assumed responsibility for the branch. As withdrawal depleted the ranks of the D1s, Billinton class D3 0-4-4 tanks took over, but since 1948 they in turn were succeeded by *ex*-LSWR class M7 0-4-4 tanks. In later years, freight traffic was handled by LBSCR classes C2X, C3 and E4, with the Southern Railway Q and Q1 classes making an occasional appearance. The C3 class, known as the Horsham Goods, became extinct in 1952. Class 33 Diesel locomotives ran to Midhurst in the last year of freight working and class 08 Diesel shunters operated most goods services to Petworth in that station's final year.

The LSWR section of the line was worked by Beattie tanks in the early days, but for many years Adams class T1 0-4-4 tanks predominated; one was stabled in the LSWR shed at Midhurst, a sub-shed to Fratton. This shed was closed in 1937, after which the branch was worked by class M7 0-4-4 tanks from Guildford shed.

Pulborough towards Midhurst

... TRAVEL TO ...

MIDHURST

BY THE

Brighton Railway

CHEAP DAY EXCURSIONS
June to September, 1910.

SUNDAYS.		MONDAYS.		RETURN FARE 3rd class
By train leaving at	FROM	By train leaving at	FROM	
A.M.		A.M.		**3/6**
7 0	London Bridge ...	6 35	London Bridge ...	
7 6	New Cross ...	6 20	Victoria	
6 53	South Bermondsey ...	6 9	Kens'gt'n (Addi'n.rd.)	*3/- from
7 7	Peckham Rye ...	6 11	West Brompton ...	these
7 10	East Dulwich ...	6 13	Chelsea and Fulham ...	Stations.
7 0	Victoria	6 16	Battersea	On Bank
7 8	Clapham Junction ...	6 27	Clapham Junction ...	Holiday the
6 49	Balham	6 20	Mitcham Junction ...	Fare will be
7 23	*Norwood Junction ...	6 42	*Wallington	increased.
7 37	*East Croydon ...	7 1	*Sutton	

Returning from Midhurst 6.45 p.m. on Sundays, and 7.51 p.m. on Mondays.

WEEK-END CHEAP RETURN TICKETS

are issued EVERY FRIDAY, SATURDAY & SUNDAY from
LONDON BRIDGE, VICTORIA, KENSINGTON (*Addison Rd.*)
and certain Suburban Stations—

FARES :—*1st class* 16/-   *2nd class* 10/6.   *3rd class* 8/6.

available to return by any train (according to class) on Sunday,
Monday or Tuesday only.

London Bridge Terminus,
June, 1910.

WILLIAM FORBES,
General Manager.

PULBOROUGH

The first four pictures and several others in this book were taken by the late E. Wallis in the 1920's. At the time he was a signal engineer on the Southern Railway and amongst his interests were photography and his work. We can enjoy the results of this twin interest but must make allowance for his camera lens (which gave some distortions at the edges) and the almost complete lack of trains (which presumably spoilt a picture of trackwork in the eyes of a signal engineer).

Pulborough looking south in April 1923 with the rear view of a train to the South Coast in down platform. The only locomotive in the picture is a traction engine in the goods yard. The goods shed is behind the up starting signal, whilst, the platform for Midhurst trains is obscured by the signal box.

This view of Pulborough looking north towards London in May 1923 was taken from the top of the up home signal, just visible in the background of the picture opposite. The loop line platform was the terminating point for most trains from Midhurst. The large tank for locomotive water can be seen beyond the loop line.

A close-up view of the up siding shunt signal taken on the same day as the l[a]
picture. Details to note are the white water level indicators on the side of the ta
and branch line engine taking on water from the column by the up starting sign
The stack of coal was for locomotives as the LBSCR engine shed at Midhurst w
closed at about this time.

Signalman E. Shepperd poses for the signal engineer on 17th May 1923.

Ex LBSCR Class D1 Tank, No. B357, in Southern livery, arriving at Pulborough with the Midhurst branch train in August 1930. This locomotive, built in 1886 at Brighton was formerly named "Riddlesdown" and, together with eight others of this class, was fitted as a locomotive fire engine in 1941 for use at large railway yards during bombing raids. A ton of water a minute could be discharged through four jets. It was broken up in 1947.

(H.C. Casserley)

Looking south after the 1938 electrification but probably before station nameboards were removed for the duration of the war. The old style nameboards were generally replaced by enamelled metal signs after the war but Southern Railway target signs can be seen further down the platform.

(Lens of Sutton)

A typical scene as Ex-LSWR M7 Class locomotive No. 30050 arrives at Pulborough station with a push-pull set from Midhurst, 14th April 1954.

(P. Hay)

The last scheduled train to Petworth leaves Pulborough yard on the 20th May 1966 made up of two coal wagons with the last delivery of coal to Petworth yard and two brake vans; one for the guard and Area Manager, and the other to accommodate three railway enthusiasts. An unscheduled trip was made the following week to collect empty wagons.

(J.A.M. Vaughan)

Hardham Junction was the point at which the Midhurst branch left the Mid-Sussex line to the south coast and turned westward to the first station at Fittleworth. The signal box was the last survivor of the LBSCR 'Box on Stilts' type and was removed soon after the closure of the branch. This view was taken from the train seen in the previous photograph as it ran 'wrong line' from the crossover and the single line token was collected. A point blade can be seen below the signalman's hand.

(J.A.M. Vaughan)

Q Class Locomotive No. 30545 approaches Fittleworth on a fine summer day in June 1962. Many crews regarded a week's turn on the Midhurst line as something of a holiday and this photograph certainly confirms the view. The signal is Hardham junction fixed distant and was the the only signal left on the branch in the "goods only" days.

(R.A. Holder)

FITTLEWORTH

Porter J. Tulett poses for E. Wallis. This little box, with its charming roof finial, was demolished in 1931 and replaced by a ground frame which was unlocked by the single line token. Tulett started work at this station in 1915 when there was a station master, booking clerk and three porters. He retired in 1963 when the station closed.

Although the railway had passed through Fittleworth since 1859 it was not until 30 years later that the village had a station of its own, opened in the September of 1889 in response to local pressure led by Sir Walter Barttelot, M.P. This photograph taken by Walter Kevis, at about the time of opening, shows the simple design of the wooden building built at a cost of little over £1,000 by a Mr. Cook.

(Garland Collection)

A Red Cross exercise in progress in the station yard and Fittleworth's first taxi waits outside the station for a fare in 1913. We feel the rarity of views outside the station justifies the inclusion of occasional photographs that have suffered in earlier reproductions or the passage of time.

(Courtesy Mrs. G.J. Smith)

A Christmas Card scene! Fittleworth under snow in January 1958.

(R.A. Holder)

Fittleworth goods yard seen in August 1958 shows only a few coal wagons although up to a 1,000 tons of sugar beet would be loaded here after the harvest. Coal was delivered locally by horse and cart from this yard as late as 1966, but it arrived by road after May 1963, when freight facilities here were withdrawn.

(B.C. Vigor)

Push-pull set No. 737 propelled by M7 Class Locomotive No. 30050 arrives at Fittleworth with the Pulborough-Petersfield train on the 14th April 1954. We have not been able to find an explanation for the considerable gap between the station canopy and the platform edge.

(P. Hay)

Class E4 Locomotive No. 32469 passes through Fittleworth in April 1960, with the Midhurst to Horsham goods. In LBSCR days this engine was named "Beachy Head".

(D. Cross)

The last scheduled goods from
Petworth passes the old yard at
Fittleworth. Although Fittleworth
yard had only closed three years
earlier, the track had been lifted,
and the track bed was already
becoming overgrown.

Note that the platform canopy
supports are beginning to sink.

(J.A.M. Vaughan)

Evidence of the travelling habits of one passenger, found in the Midhurst Times of 29 October 1897.

91 years after opening, the old building refuses to give in, even though rapidly being taken over by nature.

(D. Dornom)

PETWORTH

This is the original Petworth Station opened in 1859, photographed by Walter Kevis in 1889 just before its demolition. The top hatted Station Master, Mr. Chapman, holding the single line staff, appears to be watching the arrival of a train from Pulborough, in this very obviously posed shot. The station name is picked out in white stones opposite the platform and the roofs of three wooden built cottages for Railway employees can be seen beyond the signal box.   The water column is on the extreme right.

◄—————— Two superb photographs of the new Petworth station, again taken by Walter Kervis in 1892 and found in the Garland collection. This would have been shortly after the opening performed by the Duke of Connaught, who was staying at Petworth House with a shooting party. The glass in the roof was obviously still clean, to have illuminated the posters so clearly.

Petworth goods yard about the turn of the century. In the background can be seen the pumping house and at the right of this is a wooden built cottage, known in later years as 'Granny Clarks' Cottage (Grandad Clark was ganger on the line). It is reputed to have been the original West Norwood station.

(Courtesy A. Flexman)

◄—————— The carriage drive of the new station. An obvious effort had been made by the architect to achieve a building far more ornate than the usual wooden structures.

The house on the hill behind the station, was the residence of the station master.

In bygone days it was not unusual for whole farms to be moved by Railway Companies. This photograph, taken in October 1933, shows a train of GWR wagons arriving at Petworth loaded with farm stock and implements.

It will be noticed that the platform canopy had by now been shortened. The work was carried out in 1932 after the discovery of a bees nest in the woodwork at the western end.   So much wood had to be removed, it was decided to shorten the canopy. The eastern end was then cut away to match. (G. Garland)

Few signal boxes were in a position to bear so many enamelled advertisement signs and their presence distracts one from the flaking box name. The signal engineer's tool bag is below the first Whitbread's sign.

(Late E. Wallis)

Percy Ayling on duty in Petworth Signal Box in 1955. This box contained an 18 lever frame and was a typical **LBSCR** design. It was closed in December 1957 but not demolished until much later.

(C. White)

The last goods train from Petworth, headed by a 350hp Diesel Shunter, waits to leave on the 20th May 1966. The remaining few items of furniture from the Station office are being loaded into the guards van.

(J.A.M. Vaughan)

An unusually clean M7 Class Locomotive No. 30050 leaves with a twin push-pull unit for Pulborough – 14th April 1954.

(P. Hay)

The view from the guards van as the last goods train leaves
Petworth Station. Although the occasion was only witnessed
by a few people, the customary detonators were placed on
the metals to mark the end of 106 years of service. Petworth
Station the first to open, was the last to close.

(J.A.M. Vaughan)

A burst culvert near Selham, Boxing Day 1886. Repairs were ——→
carried out by building up the embankment with chalk
removed from a fall near West Dean Tunnel on the
Chichester-Midhurst line.

(C. White Collection)

SELHAM

good view of the simple wooden station, opened in 1872. The two nearest lamps are now in use
the house of one of the authors, whilst the other is in the possession of a collector in Hampshire.
(Lens of Sutton)

M7 No. 30328 pulls away from Selham with a Petersfield to Pulborough train on 15th October 1950.

(S.C. Nash)

The diminutive signal box stood at the west end of the platform and is shown here in front of a crowded goods yard on 18th September 1923, prior to closure in 1933.

(Late E. Wallis)

Q Class Locomotive No. 30536 pauses at Selham shortly before the withdrawal of goods services from this station in May 1963.

The platform lamp in the foreground had already been removed, but the cattle dock on the left still remains.

(C. White)

"Sussex Coast Ltd" Rail-tour double headed by E4 Class No. 32503 and E6 Class No. 32417 passes through Selham, having visited Midhurst on the 24th June 1962.

The station approach road is obscured by the locomotives in this view but the separate roadway to the cattle dock can be seen on the left of the picture. Few stations had the luxury of segregated approaches which must have been a blessing to passengers footwear on dark nights when beyond the illumination of the station's paraffin lamps.

(R.A. Holder)

Petersfield towards Midhurst

L. & S. W. R.
(LONDON AND SOUTH WESTERN RAILWAY).

The Picturesque Route

TWO HOURS' JOURNEY
only, from
LONDON
(Waterloo Station) to

MIDHURST

By Portsmouth Direct Line through the charming scenery of the Surrey Hills

CHEAP RETURN TICKETS FROM LONDON
(Waterloo Station) as under:—

WEEK-END.—1st, 16/-: 2nd, 10/6: 3rd, 8/6, by all trains.

EXCURSION.—3/6 (Day) and 7/6 (Period) issued on certain days during the Summer only.

EXPRESS CORRIDOR TRAINS,
Breakfast, Luncheon & Dining Cars

between LONDON (Waterloo) & BOURNEMOUTH,
. . SWANAGE, WEYMOUTH, ILFRACOMBE, . .
. . EXETER, SIDMOUTH, PADSTOW, BUDE, . .
. . PLYMOUTH, and other places in the . .

SOUTH AND WEST OF ENGLAND

For full particulars of Train Service, Cheap Tickets, see pamphlets obtainable at the Company's Stations and Offices, or from

MR. HENRY HOLMES, *Supt.* of the LINE, WATERLOO STATION, S.E.

CHAS. J. OWENS, *General Manager.*

← Steam was almost universal traction on the lines to Midhurst so this is an unusual photograph. A Class 33 Diesel locomotive crossing Ambersham Common between Midhurst and Selham on the 5th August 1964.
(R.A. Holder)

1955.

Looking south from the footbridge of Petersfield station. Had it not been for the mist on the November day in 1923 when this view was taken, the fine panorama of the South Downs could have been seen. Trains to Midhurst sometimes started from the platform on the loop, especially if there were heavy parcels to be loaded such as boxes of fish, as was usually the case with the 7.41 a.m. departure in later years.

The signalbox adjacent to the level crossing seen on the same November day. A smaller box existed to the south of the station controlling entry to the numerous sidings on both sides of the main line. (The late E. Wallis photos)

PETERSFIELD JUNCTION

PETERSFIELD

The northward view from the footbridge shows the main road to Winchester in the foreground and the branch junction with the electrified main line from London in the background. The single line to Midhurst is the one on the left under the bridge, the other being a siding to the ITS rubber factory.

(Lens of Sutton)

Class M7 locomotive No. 30050 with a twin push-pull set waits to return to Pulborough on 14th April 1954. Behind the train is a short siding and the dairy, the latter receiving some of the milk conveyed along the branch although much of it was destined for London.

(P. Hay)

Passengers to Midhurst usually had to trudge across the main road to this wooden shelterless platform. The lattice footbridge can be seen behind the telegraph pole. The life of the branch was near its end when this M7 and push-pull coach was pictured.

(L. & G.R.P. Collection, Courtesy David & Charles)

The Ordnance Survey map of 1879 shows that at Petersfield the station was separated from the small town by fields. Victorian urban development largely filled in these open spaces in the 1860's, Cowlegs Lane becoming Station Road, although curiously this runs over the level crossing, whilst Lavant Street was the name chosen for the street to the station.

"The Hampshireman" coming off the branch at Petersfield onto the down main line on Sunday 6th February 1955. This was a farewell tour, organised by the RCTS, of the Midhurst lines and the Meon Valley route, all of which had closed to passengers the previous day. The locomotives running bunker to bunker are E5X Nos. 32576 and 32570.

(K. Smith Collection)

ROGATE

A fine view looking towards Petersfield taken from a postcard dated 1912. At this time there were two functional platforms and full signalling.

(Courtesy E. Ayling)

Looking east towards Midhurst one of the two sidings can be seen together with part of the small goods shed, situated between the signal box and station. The shed was built of second-hand sleepers on end and was roofed with corrugated iron sheets.

(Lens of Sutton)

Former LSWR Class M7 No. 30050 arrives at Rogate with a Petersfield-Pulborough train, 14th April 1954.

There was no platform canopy here or at Elsted but the LSWR did provide one at its Midhurst terminus. To the right of the locomotive is the chimney and shear legs of a sawmill.

Former LBSCR Class E4 No. 32464 leaves Rogate for Petersfield on the same day with a non-existent freight train. The siding in the foreground served the Nyewood brickworks, bringing coal in and taking bricks out, one large consignment surprisingly being exported to Canada. Nyewood was a small community that developed around the station which stood half way between the villages shown on its nameboard.

(Photos P. Hay)

The station building was identical to Rogate but was on the north side of the track. The double doors and adjacent windows (not round headed) enclosed a waiting area with a long built-in bench. This wooden protection was clearly provided as an afterthought at both stations. The small goods shed here was clad entirely with corrugated iron and provided with a massive ventilator much loved by many Victorian architects.

(V. Mitchell collection)

ELSTED

Class M7 No. 30028 arrives with a train from Petersfield. 104 locomotives of this class were built by the LSWR between 1897 and 1911 mainly for service in the London suburbs and most of them finished their days on rural branches.

(A. W. Burges)

Nearest the camera is a more than usually generous array of fire buckets and behind which is the "gentlemens" with half bricks missing to facilitate ventilation. Sanitary engineers at the time usually left half the roof off for this purpose but at these stations the water tank stood on a complete flat roof. The Ladies Waiting Room had the luxury of the only bay windows on the premises.

(Lens of Sutton)

The late Mr. Pretty, Ganger at Elsted for many years, sets off on his regular inspection of the permanent way and fences, which were also his responsibility.

(C. White)

Chichester towards Midhurst

LONDON BRIGHTON & SOUTH COAST RAILWAY.

NOTICE TO ENGINE DRIVERS, GUARDS, SIGNALMEN, AND ALL CONCERNED.

OPENING OF THE

Chichester and Midhurst Line

On MONDAY, July 11th, 1881.

The Line is Single, being a continuation of the Single Line, Pulborough and Midhurst. It will be worked under the Rules and Regulations for working Single Lines by Train Staff and Train Ticket, and the Block Telegraph System of Signalling for Single Lines.

The Stations on the New Line are Lavant, Singleton, and Cocking.

The Line will be called Down from Midhurst to Chichester, and Up the reverse way.

DISTANCES.

The distances between the Stations are as follows :

	M.	C.
Chichester to Lavant ...	3	31
Lavant to Singleton ...	3	13
Singleton to Cocking ...	3	2
Cocking to Midhurst ...	2	32

CHICHESTER

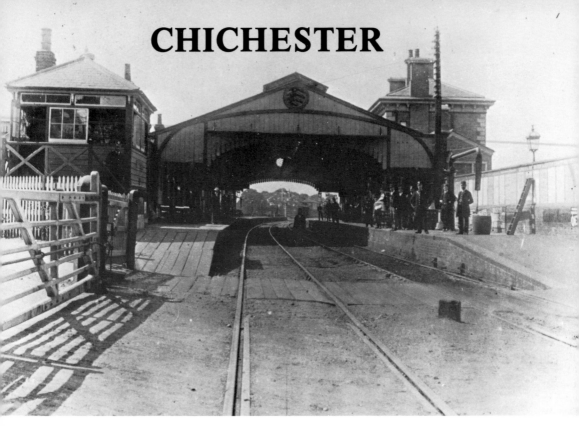

This is the only view of the overall roof we have seen and probably dates from the 1880s. The two signalboxes shown here were opened on 24 October 1875 and replaced one that was sited near the east box on the left of this picture. (Wallis collection)

LBSCR station staff at Chichester in 1913. (Courtesy L.C.G. Holden)

Looking east from the **West** Signalbox in February 1923 we see in the foreground the exchange siding with the West Sussex Railway, more commonly known as the Selsey Tramway, and at the far end of the dividing fence the white painted terminal building of that line is just apparent. The turntable was only 45 ft. diameter and with the advent of larger locomotives a turning triangle was built later to the north of the main line. The neare st signal is the starter for the Midhurst bay. The extensive cattle pens were fully utilised on Chichester market days.

Looking west from the down platform

Chichester East box controlled the South Street level crossing mechanically. Footbridge users had the comfort of a roof and railway passengers also had the use of a subway between platforms.

Everything in this photograph has now gone, except the main line to Brighton. On the left is the Police Station which was also situated opposite the railway stations at Midhurst, presumably so that the "comings and goings" could be observed. It was also a good location for communciation via the railway telegraph service, prior to the introduction of telephones.

Beyond the crossover is the Basin Road crossing which was operated by a man on foot until 1973, when both crossings received lifting barriers.

(All four photos were taken by E. Wallis, the last three on 27 April 1924)

A view westwards from the foot-bridge in January 1951 showing the original buildings of 1846 and a telegraph pole apparently sprouting from the roof behind the water column.

(Courtesy L.C.G. Holden)

An eastward view of Chichester station prior to rebuilding in 1957/8. Notable on the right are the gaslight, locomotive water tower and train for "all stations and halts to Portsmouth & Southsea". For many years this hourly service started from the bay here.

(Lens of Sutton)

Part of the rebuilt station in 1980 which had been planned before the war. John Hoare in "Sussex Railway Architecture" describes it as an outstanding example of a public building and that it seems unlikely that its quality will be equalled in any station building in the foreseeable future.

(D. Dornom)

Looking towards Portsmouth from the down yard we see (from left to right) two goods lines, down main, up main, Midhurst line (for reversible running) and the up goods yard in which there was a Lancashire and Yorkshire Railway wagon. The footbridge still exists, linking the College of Technology with the Terminus Road Industrial Estate.

Fishbourne crossing in 1927 showing the single Midhurst line diverging from the double track to Havant after crossing the road to Portsmouth. Note ornamental sewer vent pipe complete with weather vane.

(3 views — Late E. Wallis)

Q Class Locomotive No. 30532 approaching Lavant with an up goods in July 1961
at the site of the subsequent terminal for gravel trains.

(R.A. Holder)

Q Class Locomotive No. 30536, running tender first on a down sugar beet train, just south of Brandy Hole Lane Bridge, Chichester, in October 1962.

(R.A. Holder)

Most Branch lines closed to passenger traffic were visited by 'Specials' and Chichester to Lavant was no exception. Here is "The Hayling Farewell Rail Tour" in November 1963, double headed by Q Class Locomotives Nos. 30531 and 30543.

Another railway enthusiast's special to visit Lavant was "The Vectis Farewell Railtour" on 3 October 1965, headed by Q1 Class No. 33020, one of a class of 40 austerity locomotives built by O.V. Bulleid in World War II.

(Both R.A. Holder)

LAVANT

South of Lavant Station the track was diverted in 1972 to take it under a gravel hopper. In 1980 18 trains weekly each of 900 tons gross ran from Lavant to a processing plant east of Chichester.

(D. Dornom)

Lavant signalbox pictured here in 1924, had 16 levers but no passing loop to control, although loops did exist at different times.

(Late E. Wallis)

When the line was opened in 1881 the engineer, Frederick Banister, arranged for a complete set of photographs to be taken of all the civil engineering structures and the stations, with full staff. Part of that series is reproduced in this album with the permission of the West Sussex Reference Library. Lavant, along with the other stations between Chichester and Midhurst, was designed by .L. Myers. All were most ornate in appearance with mock Tudor timber framing, and flower designs in relief on the plaster. In later years all of the stations, with the exception of Cocking, had peen partially tile hung in an attempt to combat damp.

A train of sugar beet wagons passes under the main road at Lavant hauled by Class C2X No. 32550. The additional dome on this locomotive was for top feed boiler arrangements at one period during its life.

The two staircases and luggage chute had long since been removed and small offices built under the platform canopy when these two photographs were taken on 15th October 1955, by S.C. Nash.

Goods traffic nominally continued as far as Cocking until 26th August 1953, not 1957 as misprinted in Paul Clark's otherwise excellent book "The Chichester and Midhurst Railway". This well researched scholarly work is essential reading for students of this line. Sanitary engineers will be impressed by the pair of vent pipes on the end of the building which surprisingly do not appear in the 1881 photograph.

This view shows a single-domed class C2X Locomotive arriving at Lavant with an up goods, prior to the re-instalation of the platform loop in 1953.

(Lens of Sutton)

Billinton designed 0-6-2T E4 Class Locomotive No. 32509 shunts at Lavant in 1958.
   The whole class was scrapped by 1963 except No. 473 "Birch Grove" which has been preserved by the Bluebell Railway.

(A. W. Burges)

1951 WORKING TIMETABLE

Chichester		9.30
Lavant	a.	9.42
	d.	10.17
Singleton	a.	10.27
	d.	10.50
Cocking	a.	11.02
	d.	11.22
Midhurst		11.30

The limit of the concrete platform covering for sugar beet
loading shows well in this
picture taken on 3rd August
1968, — the day of closure of
Lavant station. A 350hp Diesel
shunter approaches the last
train to leave the station.
(J.A.M. Vaughan)

SINGLETON

Three engineers photographs of Singleton station in 1881. The most splendid of all Stations on th branch, lavish to the extreme, was obviously constructed with an eye to the lucrative Goodwoc traffic. From right to left — the station master's house, booking hall, ladies room, covered wa leading to the subway to the platforms and gents toilet block.

Looking north, with new staff posing on the platforms, and the goods shed in the distance. Th station was built on the side of a hill and consequently the platforms are at the level of the roof of th station master's house on the right. Situated on the down platform was a magnificent Refreshme Room complete with marble counter.

ven the goods shed was well ornamented. Between it and the North Box can be seen the docks used
r horse boxes which were so numerous during Goodwood Races that some had to be unloaded at
avant. The two island platforms on the right of this view were crowded on race days and almost
serted for the rest of the year.

THE ROYAL TRAIN

lass B4 Locomotive No. 60 "Kimberley" with a Royal Train at Singleton following the visit of King
dward VII to West Dean House. Under one of the bowler hats is Mr. J. Richardson, Outdoor
comotive Superintendent of the LBSCR.

(P. Hay collection)

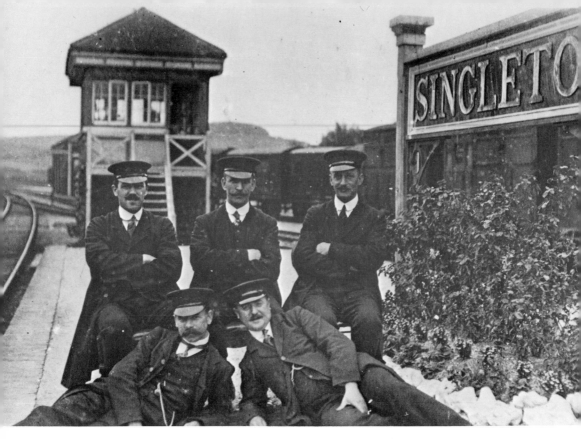

Staff at Singleton in the early days of 'Southern Railway'. In the background is the North box and beyond, the goods shed. When the station staff was later reduced to one porter/signalman/booking clerk it was necessary for him to walk from this box to the South box to set the signals for the passage of every train. North box had 28 levers whilst South box had 26.

(Lens of Sutton)

Looking north at Singleton in 1947. Despite its derelict appearance there was still a heavy goods traffic — mostly timber and agricultural produce outward — coal and fertiliser inward. The disused waiting room on the right-hand platform was used as the goods office. (L. & G.R.P. Collection, courtesy David & Charles)

Looking south from near the south signal box showing the locomotive water tower and the mouth of West Dean tunnel before the closure of the boxes on 8th October 1933, nearly 2 years before passenger trains ceased.

(C.W.G. Allaston)

Singleton station is now the home of the Chilsdown Vineyard. The station house provide
accommodation for the Paget family who planted their first vines in 1972. The booking hall an
waiting rooms have been utilised for wine making, bottling etc., The extra large lavatory block
formerly housing 6 WC's and 10 urinals, has a special role as the bottled wine store.

During summer months tours around the vineyard are usually possible. In addition to th
pleasure of sampling the wine, the tour starts with an introduction to the unique history of th
station.

(D. Dornom

COCKING

Cocking station, constructed in 1880 and opened in 1881. The first Station Master, Henry Chapman, complete with Top Hat, poses outside his new station for the line engineer's photographer.

At the age of 20 he earned £1-8-0 per week from which 4 shillings rent was deducted for the station house.

He moves through the booking hall to pose at the platform edge whilst his staff of porter (10/- a week) and porter-signalman (18/-) take up positions of action. The line climbs south at 1 in 60 into Cocking tunnel, which penetrates the South Downs, and can be seen in the distance.

Cocking station looking north before the Signal Box was closed in 1930. The staff were withdrawn from 1932, reducing Cocking station to a Halt. Passenger traffic ceased on the 6th July 1935.

Another engineers view, this time the north portal of Cocking tunnel with a curious skew underbridge, having only 8 feet headroom, in the foreground. This was to accommodate the extension of a siding towards Crypt farm, but could have only permitted the passage of open wagons drawn up by horse or descending by gravity.

Cocking station in the early sixties, after closure of the branch.
The covered platform made an ideal clothes drying area.

(Lens of Sutton)

Cocking station closed completely on the 28th August 1953 along with Singleton. It then passed into private ownership. The present occupants have done an enormous amount of restoration on the building as this photograph of the porch shows. A major addition has been some rooms above the former booking hall. The flower motifs in the rendering and panels are common to all the stations between Chichester and Midhurst.

(P. Clark)

D Class Tank No. 239 'Patcham' came to grief on Friday 9th September 1904 between Cocking and Midhurst when, for no apparent reason, it left the rails, taking with it an open truck, box van and guards van. It was finally lifted back onto the rails two days later. (P. Boulding collection)

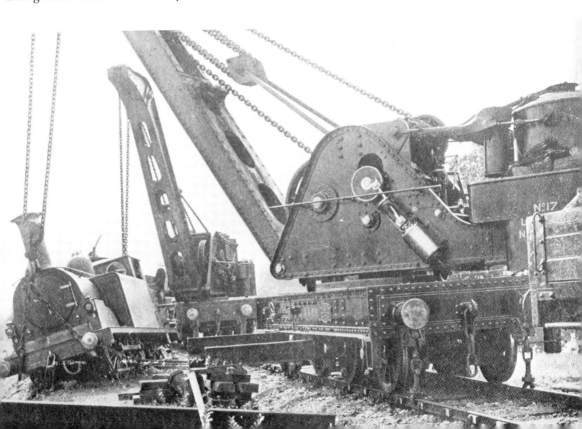

On the 19th November, 1951, Class C2X No. 32522 fell into a stream swollen by torrential rain between Cocking and Midhurst while in charge of the 9.30 a.m. goods from Chichester. The bridge had collapsed into the stream earlier; fortunately the Bognor crew noticed the sagging rails ahead and just managed to jump clear. The entire contents of the coal bunker, about 3 tons, cascaded onto and around the footplate where it promptly caught fire close to the open firebox door, and in turn set alight the 10 tons being gravity-fed from the crushed wagon poised overhead. As the engine was clear of the water the fire burned for over a week, and was still smouldering on 2nd December, 1951 when the cab showed clear signs of its earlier intensity. Break-down cranes from Brighton and Portsmouth were called to the scene, but could only salvage the wagons, for no support could be found to take the weight of the tender, let alone the C2X. It was only after the embankment was removed for several hundred yards towards Cocking and a length of temporary track laid that No. 32522 was eventually hauled up the incline by Kelbus tackle and towed away to Brighton Works for repair.

(Photo S.C. Nash. Text RCTS)

Midhurst - - -

In the foreground is the 10 chain radius curve which necessitated placing a 20 m.p.h. speed restriction on Chichester trains. To the left are the lines to the goods yard and the freight only connection to Petersfield.

The signalman's eye view of the platforms from the **west** box (seen in the centre of the upper picture). The signals on the right were altered a few months later to permit passenger trains to run to Petersfield from this station. The quarry in the background was operated by the railway company and is shown in more detail in the next view. February 1925

Still looking east, this time from the end of the down platform, we see the single line to Petworth enter the tunnel and a steam drag-line loading wagons with sand. This quarry face is the cause of an abrupt incline in a modern road named "The Fairway". The map and pictures opposite, illustrate the rural location of the station, remote from the small town.

All the stations on the LSWR branch were similar with the exception of Midhurst, which had an additional bedroom for the station master's family and the platform had a canopy. The extra room, in the centre of this picture, appears to be a later addition judging by the joint in the brickwork and the differing ridge tiles.

The platform of the LSWR terminus is made of timber where the milk churns are standing, being a durable resilient material to bear the impact of these heavy items when being unloaded from farmer's carts backed into the hollow behind the lamp post. The weak bridge over the Bepton Road can be seen on the through line near the LBSCR buffer stops. That company's locomotive shed is just visible behind the stabled coach. Note the catch point this side of the bridge to derail vehicles intruding from the rival firm's territory.

The LSWR signalbox, photographed in November 1923, was closed in July 1925 and later moved to Easebourne where it stood in retirement as a summer house.

Midhurst South box (LBSCR) was at the east end of the up platform and went out of use on 4 April 1925, later becoming the station master's office. The last seven views were taken on 18 February 1925 (except the LSWR signal box) by the signal engineer, E. Wallis.

L.B.S.C.R. Signal Boxes at Midhurst

Midhurst South Box
(also known as East Box)

The rear view of these boxes was
similar to the front view, except
that there was plain planking in
place of windows.

Scale 2mm to 1ft.

Midhurst North Box
(also known as West Box)

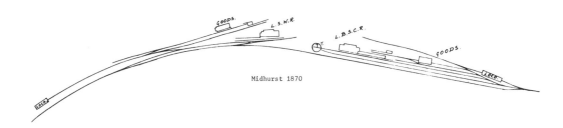

Midhurst 1870

L.B.S.C.R. Midhurst station

North elevation

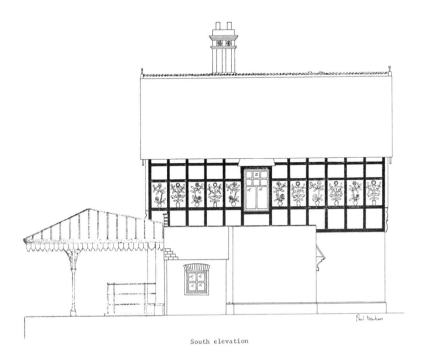

South elevation

Scale 2mm to 1ft.

Platform elevation

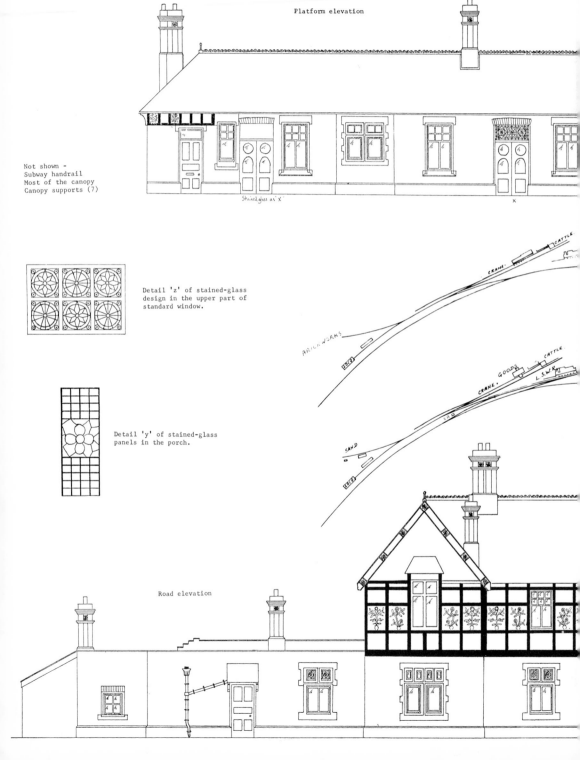

Not shown -
Subway handrail
Most of the canopy
Canopy supports (7)

Stained glass as 'X'

X

Detail 'z' of stained-glass
design in the upper part of
standard window.

Detail 'y' of stained-glass
panels in the porch.

Road elevation

BRICKWORKS

CRANE

CATTLE

CRANE

GOODS

CATTLE

L.S.W.R.

SAND

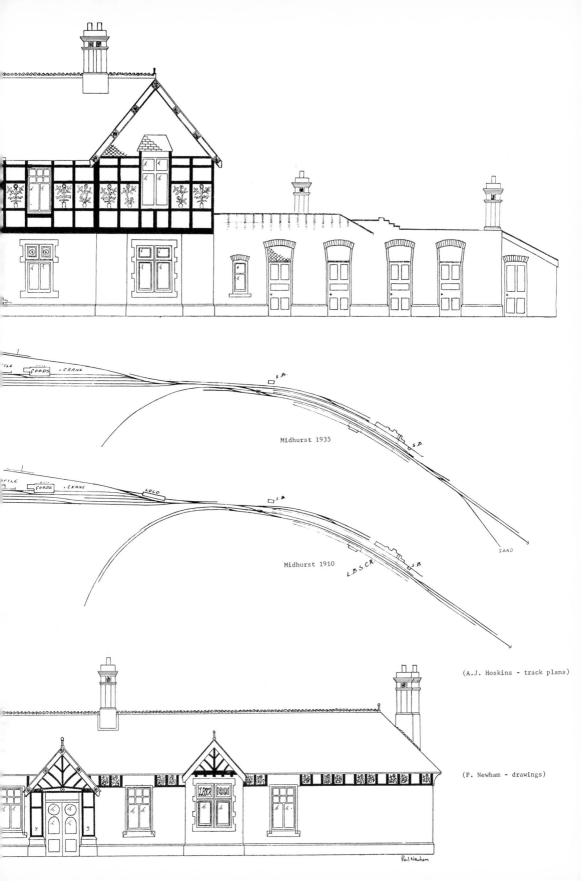

Midhurst 1935

Midhurst 1910

L.B.S.C.R.

FOODS · CRANE

LOCO

SAND

(A.J. Hoskins - track plans)

(P. Newham - drawings)

Paul Newham

M7 Class Locomotive No. 130 with a single coach waits to start from the bay platform with the Petersfield train on the 30th October 1928. Through trains between Chichester and Pulborough used the other two platforms at this time.

Former LSWR Locomotive T1 Class No. 75 stands in the Petersfield Bay on 30th August 1930 a few minutes after the cover photograph had been taken. Note the unusual orientation of the nameboards on the lamp posts.

(Photos H.C. Casserley)

Ex LSWR Jubilee
Class A12 0-4-2
No. 631 stands
in   Midhurst
goods yard.
       (Courtesy
    G. Evans)

This is the first **LBSCR** locomotive shed at Midhurst
and shows considerable settlement on the south side,
a condition which the west signal box also suffered in
later years. This shed was replaced in 1907 by another
wooden structure which appears in the cover photograph. On the left is the original goods shed and
beyond it the replacement shed with characteristic
circular window.   (Lens of Sutton)

Ex LSWR T1 Class 0-4-4T No. 75 passes Midhurst West box in August 1930 whilst running round its train from Petersfield which was standing in the bay platform. Most trains on this branch terminated in the bay between 1925 and 1935. The signal box had 47 levers and was in use from the opening of the Chichester line in 1881 until after the cessation of passenger services in 1955. There are many interesting details in this westward looking view — in the left foreground the other two platform roads merge and curve left towards Cocking whilst in the far distance the disused former LSWR station can be discerned on the extreme left. To its right is the ex-LBSCR goods shed, engine shed and water tower, the latter partially obscured by the signal post and gas lamp, a loading gauge in the middle distance and a glimpse of New Road, which is mentioned in the introduction.

(H.C. Casserley)

M7 Class Locomotive No. 30328 with a single unit passes the remains of the LSWR Engine shed in April 1953 **in** mist.

The shed, a single ended brick built structure with a water tank over the doors, closed completely in 1937. (S.C. Nash)

The Station Master and staff pose outside the former Midhurst South box. From left to right, Messrs. Pullen (Booking Clerk), Dymond (Station master), Tiller (Signalman) and Pearce (Delivery Lorry Driver) February 1955. (C. White)

Push-pull set No. 731 waits to leave for Pulborough during the last few days of passenger traffic. Examples of the regular traffic are visible — some milk churns by the fence, a few mailbags, a couple of parcels — and passengers are typically invisible. However, some architectural detail is worth noting in this fine quality photograph.

Class M7 No. 30049 about to leave for Pulborough with a train strengthened to three coaches for the extra traffic on one of the last days of ordinary passenger services. The missing bricks above the passenger's head are, in this case, for the ventilation of the lamp room.   (C. White)

The ill fated class C2X No. 32522, that we last saw boiler deep in mud, shunts at Midhurst after an extensive rebuild at Brighton Locomotive Works. Its odd looking tender was made up from the chassis of a scrapped C2X and the body of a former LSWR T9 tender.

Re-railing Class E5X No. 32570 in Midhurst Yard.

Note the unusual handrail around the dome.

These three photographs were taken by Charles White, a professional photographer in Midhurst for most of his career. Whilst he was waiting to photograph the arrival of a train from Pulborough on the last day of passenger services this beautiful creature appeared from the tunnel instead of the train, which accounted for the prolonged whistling that had been heard earlier, beyond the hill.

Midhurst Tunnel (East End)
1961 E4 No. 32470
1960 C2X No. 32523

(R.A. Holde
(D. Cros

During August 1958 Midhurst Station was transformed into a film set for the making of Carlton Browne of the Foreign Office. Terrier tank No. 32640 underwent minor modifications to become 'Anna Karenina'.

(P. Hay)

A few minutes before the photograph opposite was taken, 32523 stands in the goods yard with excess steam ready to depart for Pulborough and Horsham.

(D. Cross)

Q Class locomotive No. 30530 with the joint RCTS/LCGB Special after arriving at Midhurst on the 18th October 1964. This was the last train of any type to be seen at Midhurst.

(C. White)

The only railway buildings to survive at Midhurst, apart from cottages, were the former LBSCR goods shed (at right of picture), used as a timber store, and the former LSWR station (in the distance) which after years of neglect was converted to offices.

(C. White)